UCHICAGO **Consortium**
on School Research

CONCEPT PAPER FOR RESEARCH AND PRACTICE   APRIL 2018

High School Graduation and College Readiness Indicator Systems

What We Know, What We Need to Know

Elaine M. Allensworth, Jenny Nagaoka, and David W. Johnson

TABLE OF CONTENTS

ACKNOWLEDGEMENTS

The authors gratefully acknowledge the many people who contributed to this report. It builds on the knowledge base on high school graduation and college readiness indicator systems that has grown through the contributions of many researchers, policymakers, and practitioners over time. We are especially grateful to the experts who attended our May 2016 convening: Hadar Baharav, Manuelito Biag, Jessica Cardichon, Faith Connolly, Susan Fairchild, Nate Flint, Joanna Fox, Sarah Frazelle, Carl Frederick, Jessica Heppen, Chris Mazzeo, Mark Milliron, Angela Romans, Jenny Scala, Jason Snipes, Andrew Statz, Sarah Truelsch, Jason Willis, and Kyo Yamashiro.

We thank members of UChicago Consortium's research review group, particularly Marisa de la Torre, Lauren Sartain, and Kylie Klein, as well as our external reviewers, Eliza Moeller and Alex Seeskin, for providing very valuable feedback and helping us condense a lot of information into a readable document. We also gratefully acknowledge the dedicated efforts of the communications staff at the UChicago Consortium, including Bronwyn McDaniel, Jessica Tansey, and Jessica Puller, who also provided considerable feedback to improve this report.

This work was generously funded by the Bill & Melinda Gates Foundation and we thank the Foundation for their support and the guidance from our Program Officers Eli Pristoop and Bill Tucker throughout this project. The UChicago Consortium greatly appreciates support from the Consortium Investor Council that funds critical work beyond the initial research: putting the research to work, refreshing the data archive, seeding new studies, and replicating previous studies. Members include: Brinson Family Foundation, CME Group Foundation, Crown Family Philanthropies, Lloyd A. Fry Foundation, Joyce Foundation, Lewis-Sebring Family Foundation, McCormick Foundation, McDougal Family Foundation, Osa Family Foundation, Polk Bros. Foundation, Spencer Foundation, Steans Family Foundation, and The Chicago Public Education Fund. We also gratefully acknowledge the Spencer Foundation and the Lewis-Sebring Family Foundation, whose operating grants support the work of the UChicago Consortium.

Cite as: Cite as: Allensworth, E.M., Nagaoka, J., & Johnson, D.W. (2018). *High school graduation and college readiness indicator systems: What we know, what we need to know.* Chicago, IL: University of Chicago Consortium on School Research.

This report was produced by the UChicago Consortium's publications and communications staff: Bronwyn McDaniel, Director of Outreach and Communication; Jessica Tansey, Communications Manager; and Jessica Puller, Communications Specialist.

Graphic Design: Jeff Hall Design
Photography: iStock and Pixabay
Editing: Jessica Puller and Jessica Tansey

04.2018/PDF/jh.design@rcn.com

Introduction

Increasing students' educational attainment has become a top priority for high schools across the country. Policymakers and school districts have set the ambitious goal of getting all students to graduate from high school ready to succeed in college. The outcomes that schools want to target—high school and college graduation—are the culmination of years of education. Educators have been using early warning and college readiness indicators to make assessments of which students need what kinds of support to stay on track for high school graduation and college readiness before they far too fall behind.

- **Early Warning Indicators (EWI):** Information on students' likelihood of high school graduation
  - Used to improve high school dropout and graduation rates

- **College Readiness Indicators:** Information on likelihood of obtaining a college degree
  - Used to improve students' post-secondary outcomes (enrollment, persistence, and graduation from college)

At its most basic, an indicator provides a prediction of educational attainment (e.g., high school graduation, college graduation) well in advance of the outcome. Predicting an outcome is not the same thing as knowing that outcome will occur; the prediction provides an estimate of what a student's probable outcome is so school practitioners can work to change that student's educational trajectory if the student is not likely to meet their goal. By organizing pieces of data on student performance into indicators, school practitioners can develop and test school strategies to improve students' educational attainment with data that are readily available.

While many school practitioners and policymakers embrace the use of indicators for reaching their goals around students' educational attainment, they are not always clear about how to do so in ways that will effectively lead to better educational attainment for their students. As schools, districts, and states develop systems for using indicator data, many questions have emerged, falling in two general areas:

1. *How* are indicators used to improve high school and college graduation rates?

2. *Which* indicators should be the focus of an early warning or college readiness indicator system?

The questions are intertwined. Decisions about which indicators are the best indicators to use depend on how they are being used, and questions about how to use indicators depend on the choice of indicators.

This document provides a brief overview of the current state of the use of indicators for improving students' educational attainment, considerations about which indicators to use when developing an indicator system, and some of the questions that have arisen as schools, districts, and states engage in these efforts. It is intended to support the use of indicators by summarizing the data issues and research behind high school graduation and college readiness indicator systems, and suggests lines of inquiry that are needed to support further improvements in indicator use in schools.[1] It is intended for people who are positioned between the research and practice spheres, such as district and state institutional researchers, or researchers at universities and research organizations who work closely with schools and districts. It may also be of interest to school and district administrators with a strong interest in developing and refining high school graduation and college readiness indicator systems, and an interest in the data and research behind such systems.

- **Chapter 1** provides an overview of how indicators are being used to improve students' educational outcomes.

- **Chapter 2** discusses considerations for choosing which indicators to use, and summarizes the research base around the indicators of high school graduation and college readiness that are currently in use.

- **Chapter 3** outlines some of the areas in which new research is needed, and sets priorities for research

from our perspective, highlighting four areas of work that we believe have considerable promise for improving equity in educational attainment.

Most of the examples of indicator use in this paper come from our experiences working with the Chicago Public Schools (CPS). Chicago has been using early warning and college readiness indicator systems for about a decade, and has seen considerable improvements in both high school graduation and college enrollment rates.[2] When developing the document, we sought and received valuable input from researchers and practitioners currently doing this work across the country, including the Annenberg Institute for School Reform, Baltimore Education Research Consortium, Education Northwest, Everyone Graduates Center, John W. Gardner Center, Los Angeles Education Research Institute, New Visions for Public Schools, and the REL Midwest, which guides our discussion, as well.

---

1   Much more information on the theory behind indicator systems, their uses in real school settings, and guides for practice can be found in Neild, Balfanz, & Herzog (2007); Bruce, Bridgeland, Fox, & Balfanz (2011); Allensworth (2013); Balfanz (2011); Davis, Herzog, & Legters (2013); Li, Scala, Gerdeman, & Blumenthal (2016); Fairchild, Scaramellino, Carrino, Carrano, Gunton, & Donohue (2013).

2   Nagaoka, Seeskin, & Coca (2017).

CHAPTER 1

How are Indicators Used to Improve Students' Educational Attainment?

Indicator systems often use data that are gathered as part of the regular process of education and exist within school, district, or state data systems. For example, student attendance and grades are used as indicators in many systems. Having data is not the same as having an indicator system. It is only with the strategic use of information within data systems to guide improvement of outcomes that a piece of data becomes an indicator. Decisions about how indicators will be used are essential for deciding what types of indicators to include in the system.

One way of using indicators is to identify students in need of intervention. For this purpose, indicators are usually pieces of data about individual students that are organized in an actionable way. A second way of using indicators is to focus, guide, and assess progress of school improvement efforts. For this purpose, indicators usually provide information about settings (e.g., classrooms, schools), either by aggregating data on individual students (e.g., school attendance rates) or by providing other information about the setting, such as the overall school climate. A final purpose of indicators is for the purpose of accountability—to hold schools

accountable for their students' proximal educational outcomes in advance of knowing graduation or postsecondary outcomes.[3]

Often the systems for identifying students in need of intervention, or for guiding school improvement, are highly collaborative. They bring teachers, school staff, families, and even students together around data to identify who needs what types of support, and develop plans to help keep students on the path to meeting their educational goals.[4] Thus, indicator systems can be a mechanism for increasing collaboration in the school around student-centered goals.

This chapter provides an overview of the ways in which indicators are used in schools, and some of the concerns that arise as practitioners engage in this work. The subsequent chapter then provides an illustration of the use of indicators in two districts that have received considerable support for this work—Chicago and New York. The examples highlight what this work can potentially do for improving students' attainment, and also some of the challenges that exist to doing this work without support.

What Are Early Warning or College Readiness Indicators?

Early warning or college readiness indicators are created with data that predict students' future educational attainment, and are organized to facilitate strategic action for improving student outcomes.

How are they used?
- To identify students in need of intervention
- To systematically focus, guide, and assess school improvement
- To hold schools accountable for students' outcomes

Examples
- **Student Level:** A list of ninth-graders updated weekly, flagging students with low attendance or Ds/Fs in their classes—used to identify who needs intervention
- **Setting Level:** First quarter attendance rates by period and subject—used to identify patterns in absences in the school

---

3 The John W. Gardner Center developed a framework for the College Readiness Indicator Systems Project that conceptualizes indicators at the individual student level, the setting (school or classroom) level, and the system level. The summary we provide here is consistent with that framework, but as the

focus is on the school we omit description of system-level indicators. For more information on their framework, see Borsato, Nagaoka, and Foley (2013) and Gurantz and Borsato (2012).

4 Pinkus (2008); Neild et al. (2007); Allensworth (2013).

Identifying Students in Need of Support

Effective indicator systems provide information to help educators assist students achieve long-term educational attainment goals, including high school and college graduation. Students are flagged for support before they fall too far off-track to be able to catch up.[5]

In schools without indicator systems, students can fall through the cracks when they start to struggle and fall behind. School staff's attention tends to be drawn to students with the most obvious problems, who are at a high risk of dropping out, rather than students who are struggling in less obvious ways and for whom modest interventions could prevent future problems. By intervening early, practitioners can prevent small problems, such as a few course absences, from growing into major obstacles, such as course failures and leaving school. Early intervention requires fewer resources and makes it easier for the intervention to be successful because students are not so far behind. It also reduces the number of students who eventually need substantial interventions—interventions that may have little likelihood of success.

An EWI system provides data reports on students throughout the school year, showing which students are in need of support. The system also must include structures that provide guidance to educators around data use. Because multiple adults often work with the same students, data systems can provide a bridge around which they can coordinate their efforts to support students. For example:

- Diplomas Now schools use an EWI team, where teachers and support staff review student data, assign interventions, and report back on how students are doing to the team. The EWI team can share information across multiple adults working with the same student, and provide support and guidance to each other, as well as consistent support to the student.[6]

- In Chicago, data reports are issued at regular intervals (generally every other week) that flag ninth-grade students getting Ds or below in a core course,

or with low attendance. At many high schools, ninth-grade teacher teams get together weekly or monthly around data reports. They develop strategies for reaching out to each student long before the student has failed a class for the semester or is too far behind in missed work to catch up. The teams share information about students to learn why students are struggling, and develop plans to support shared students in a coordinated way.[7] At other Chicago schools, designated staff members use midterm grades and monthly absence reports to identify students who are struggling, reaching out to the students and bringing students, parents, and teachers together to develop a strategy for getting the student back on track.

Indicators help guide supports and interventions. Good student-level indicators allow practitioners to identify which students need support, based on clear criteria, and make sure that no students who need support are overlooked. School practitioners can also use indicators to gauge the level and type of support that is needed. Ideally, the identification of students through indicator systems goes beyond simply assigning students to a particular intervention. As adults reach out to students to learn why students are struggling, they build better relationships with students and increase students' engagement in school. Students learn that they are not alone in their struggles and that adults are willing to provide support to help them succeed. This helps prevent them from struggling again in the future.

Indicators send signals to students and families about how to reach goals. School practitioners can also use indicators to provide a signal to students and their families about the performance they need to meet their educational goals. Students and their families need to know how to prepare for high school graduation and college—often they get conflicting messages or have incomplete information. For example, adults can communicate to students the importance of passing their classes to "stay on track" for graduation, or earning all

5 Balfanz (2011); Davis et al., (2013); Kautz & Zanoni (2014).

6 Corrin, Sepanik, Rosen, & Shane (2016); Davis et al. (2013).

7 Pitcher, Duncan, Nagaoka, Moeller, Dickerson, & Beechum (2016). Also see the Network for College Success Toolkit for resources used in Chicago, available at https://ncs.uchicago.edu/freshman-on-track-toolkit

There are many questions that arise as practitioners start to do this work. Often, practitioners worry about potential negative consequences of using indicators.

Two questions are frequently raised:

1. Is there a risk of labeling students as failures, rather than supporting them to be successful?

2. If adults support students when they struggle, will they come to rely on them too much?

For these and other questions, indicator use is simply too new a field to be able to provide definitive answers.

As and Bs to have the qualifications needed for college. Without the signal provided by indicators, students and families may not be clear about what is required to reach their long-term educational goals. It can seem OK to miss class now and then, or to just put in enough effort to pass, without clear benchmarks to strive toward. Good indicators should empower students and families to take control of their education. Good indicators provide clear, shared goals that school staff, families and students work together to achieve.

Indicators can communicate district priorities for supporting students to schools. District and state education agencies can use student-level indicators to communicate a set of priorities and expectations about the work in which schools should be engaged. By providing data on student indicators, districts provide a mechanism for schools to monitor and support students so they meet short-term milestones on the path to high school or college graduation. In Chicago, for example, the district provides a college planning system to schools that tracks student college applications and other steps toward college enrollment, and the Illinois Student Assistance Commission provides a system for tracking the submission of the Free Application for Federal Student Aid (FAFSA). These systems signal to high schools that they need to attend to college planning and advising, not just academic preparation.

Guiding and Assessing School Improvement in a Systematic Way

The value of strong setting-level indicators. Reaching out to individual students is a first step in using indicator data, but large scale improvement in student outcomes takes systemic solutions, rather than a student-by-student approach. Good indicators at the setting level (classroom, school) can provide information to evaluate the effectiveness of school practices aimed at improving educational attainment, providing interim data about outcomes that occur many years later (e.g., high school and college graduation). With strong setting-level indicators, school leadership teams can assess progress and judge the effectiveness of school programs and school efforts aimed at improving long-term outcomes. They can also test assumptions about what is happening in the school, helping to identify areas where school structures are not operating as expected. This focus on data can lead to changes in adult behaviors and school systems so that they are more effective in supporting students.

Setting-level indicators can be summative or formative. Summative indicators provide information at the end of the year about how well the school met its goals around the indicator. Freshman OnTrack rates in Chicago, for example, provide information to schools at the end of the year on how many of their ninth-graders

Good indicators should empower students and families to take control of their education.

By working to provide a context that is set up so that students are more likely to succeed, fewer students need a special intervention.

ended up making sufficient progress to be likely to graduate high school in four years. Schools in Chicago use this information, holistically and broken down by student subgroups, to evaluate their efforts over the prior year. However, summative indicators do not allow for quick feedback on practices. It is not efficient to wait a year to see if new school practices had the intended result. Formative setting-level indicators that are available repeatedly throughout the year allow for much more rapid feedback about whether and how practices are working so that school practitioners can continually work on improvement. For example, because attendance is strongly related to on-track rates, and attendance data is available on an ongoing basis, classroom or school-wide attendance rates can be good setting-level indicators to monitor ninth-graders' progress in a formative way. Schools can set goals around attendance, and monitor them weekly or monthly to determine whether new practices are showing improvements in those indicators.

Some setting-level indicators are developed by aggregating student-level data. When analyzing these indicators, it is often helpful to look for patterns in the data based on student characteristics (e.g., demographics, prior academic achievement) and school groupings (e.g., period, teacher, subject) to understand the dynamics of student performance. Knowing a student's race, gender, or disability status may not significantly increase the prediction of whether they will graduate, but those pieces of information aggregated at the setting level may guide decisions about potential interventions. For example, a school that has considerably higher graduation rates among their girls than their boys might monitor gender differences in ninth-grade course failure rates—an early indicator of high school graduation—to test strategies intended to reduce the gender gap in graduation. Schools may track the percentage

of students earning Fs in their ninth-grade year as a setting-level indicator, and then compare failure rates across different classes and teachers. If course failure is clustered in a few classes, interventions might be more appropriately aimed at teachers or departments, rather than individual students. On the other hand, if students are failing classes without a strong difference across subjects, the level of intervention may be more appropriately targeted at school culture and school structures. They can also use patterns in the indicators to better understand inequities in subgroup educational attainment.

Other setting-level indicators are not aggregations of student-level indicators; instead they indicate school conditions that are associated with better outcomes for students. By working to provide a context that is set up so that students are more likely to succeed, fewer students need a special intervention. For example, students entering high schools where students generally feel safe and supported tend to come to school more often and have higher grades than similar students entering schools with weaker school climates.[8] The level of safety in a school is a setting-level indicator that can be monitored. In Chicago, schools receive setting-level indicator data based on annual surveys of teachers and students. Their responses are reported out in five areas, called the five essential supports, which include students' and teachers' perceptions of safety in the school, along with indicators of the quality of instruction, teacher and parent collaboration, and leadership in the school. The survey responses have been found to be highly predictive of teacher and school performance.[9] They provide a sense of the broader context in which students and teachers are working, and have been used to guide school improvement at a setting level, rather than solely at the level of individual students.[10]

8 Allensworth & Easton (2007).

9 Allensworth, Ponisciak, & Mazzeo (2009); Kane, McCaffrey, Miller, & Staiger (2013); Bryk, Sebring, Allensworth, Luppescu, & Easton (2010).

10 Hough, Kalogrides, & Loeb (2017); Sun, Penner, & Loeb (2017).

Just as student-level indicators can be used to guide collaboration around individual students' goals, setting-level indicators can provide information to students and their families about the school's progress around common goals. This can help to make connections for families between the messages that they receive about their child and the larger efforts occurring at the school. For example, a school might regularly send out information about its progress in meeting overall attendance goals, along with a summary of research findings on the relationship between attendance and learning gains or educational attainment. This can help families make the connection between their own child's attendance, their goals for their child's educational attainment, and the broader goals of the school.

Holding Schools Accountable for Student Outcomes

Indicators are also used by districts and states to make judgments about school progress. The setting-level indicators they choose to incorporate into accountability systems communicate a set of priorities about what matters to district administrators and where they believe schools should focus efforts to improve student outcomes.[11] For example, in Chicago, when the district integrated on-track rates into the accountability system for high schools, it provided a signal that high schools should pay more attention to students' performance in the ninth-grade year. Before that, ninth grade was often seen as a year when students could make mistakes and still recover. Eventually, individual schools developed very different practices around dropout prevention than in the past, interventions that focused on preventing failures in the ninth grade. These changes have been credited with dramatic improvements in graduation rates in the district.[12] Integrating indicators into accountability systems can bring practitioners' attention to factors that they might not realize are important in the midst of myriad competing goals.

At the same time, if schools do not have strategies and means for reaching the goals that are set, accountability can create incentives for the misuse of indicators and the corruption of the data that underlie it. School practitioners may come to view indicators primarily as evaluative tools, rather than a tool for improvement, and have little motivation to maintain the quality of data or use them in a productive way. Thus, their use in accountability should be done cautiously.

In Chicago, on-track rates only improved after the district developed real-time data reports that schools could use for early intervention and guiding school improvement. Incorporating the metric into the accountability system may have encouraged schools to use the real-time data reports and change practices, but accountability by itself was not sufficient. Accountability can provide motivation to change practices, but only if schools have strategies and supports to reach the goals that are set.

Putting It All Together: How Indicators are Implemented in Practice

Improving educational attainment and reaching goals for educational equity require changing systems. This is difficult work. Strong indicator systems facilitate improvement in a number of ways: by allowing for data-informed strategies, monitoring progress, and supporting individual students. It is not just the creation of indicators that leads to better student outcomes, but also the efforts and actions of individuals in different roles that make indicators effective. As shown in **Figure 1**, policymakers, school leaders, teachers, school staff, and outside partners all play important roles in effective indicator use.

A key requirement for indicator use is a strong data system that produces setting-level and student-level indicators for schools to use in practice. This almost always requires **District and State Policymakers** to provide the resources for the technology and the personnel to produce usable indicator data. Policymakers can facilitate the use of indicators by providing staff

---

11 Turner & Coburn (2012); Colyvas (2012).
12 Roderick, Kelley-Kemple, Johnson, & Beechum (2014).

FIGURE 1

The Use of Indicators for Improving Student Outcomes

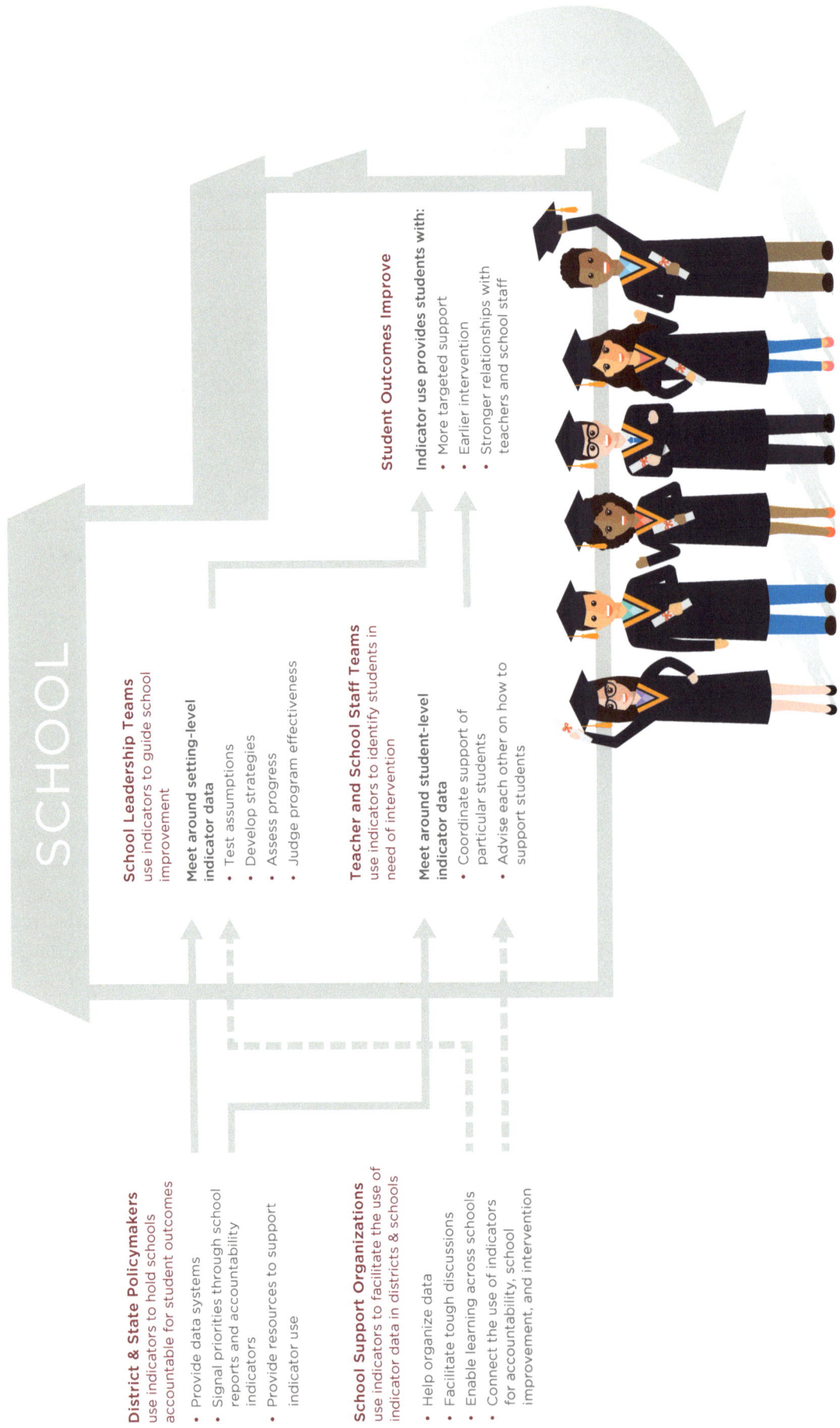

District & State Policymakers
use indicators to hold schools accountable for student outcomes

- Provide data systems
- Signal priorities through school reports and accountability indicators
- Provide resources to support indicator use

School Support Organizations
use indicators to facilitate the use of indicator data in districts & schools

- Help organize data
- Facilitate tough discussions
- Enable learning across schools
- Connect the use of indicators for accountability, school improvement, and intervention

SCHOOL

School Leadership Teams
use indicators to guide school improvement

Meet around setting-level indicator data

- Test assumptions
- Develop strategies
- Assess progress
- Judge program effectiveness

Teacher and School Staff Teams
use indicators to identify students in need of intervention

Meet around student-level indicator data

- Coordinate support of particular students
- Advise each other on how to support students

Student Outcomes Improve

Indicator use provides students with:

- More targeted support
- Earlier intervention
- Stronger relationships with teachers and school staff

who help support the use of data reports in schools, or resources that **School Support Organizations** and schools can work with around the use of indicators. District and state policymakers also decide which indicators to incorporate into accountability systems, signaling priorities to schools. Their decisions about which indicators to prioritize will influence indicator use in schools. If they focus attention on indicators that are highly predictive of educational attainment, and malleable by school practice, they are likely to see more improvements in students' educational outcomes than if they focus attention on indicators that are not predictive or malleable.

Within schools, **School Leadership Teams** use setting-level indicators to develop strategies based on indicators, and assess whether their strategies are working. The setting-level indicators may challenge their assumptions about students' progress, and this helps prompt critical discussions about what is happening in their school. At the same time, **Teacher and School Staff Teams** use the student-level indicators to identify students in need of intervention, coordinate targeted supports for students, and provide guidance and advice to each other about how to effectively engage students. This work ensures that all students who need targeted support receive it, leads students to get support earlier and in a coordinated way, and also helps build students' relationships with teachers and school staff.

Often, there is overlap between the use of **Setting-Level Indicators** around strategy and **Student-Level Indicators** around support and intervention. School

leadership may involve teachers and other school staff in strategic discussions around setting-level indicators, and to develop strategies for using student-level indicator data. And teacher-staff teams that are using student-level indicator data will develop shared and school-wide strategies to be more effective in the ways they support individual students.

While it may seem straightforward, using indicators to increase students' educational attainment ultimately requires substantial change in school practices. It takes time to organize, analyze, and reflect on the data, and then more time to figure out strategies for responding to the data.[13] Without sufficient support and training, schools often struggle to implement indicator systems.[14] In both Chicago and New York, the adoption and use of indicator systems has been facilitated by **School Support Organizations** that exist outside of the district. These intermediary organizations help schools organize data in useful ways for practice, facilitate conversations about changing school practices, and enable learning across schools about effective practices for indicator use. Because they exist outside of the school district, they can provide a safe space for reflection about school practices that would be difficult, if not impossible, for schools to do on their own or with district supervision. The box *A Profile of How School Support Organizations Facilitate the Use of Indicator Systems in Chicago and New York* on p.10 provides an overview of how two intermediary organizations have helped schools in Chicago and New York use indicators to change school practices and improve student outcomes.

---

13 Marsh (2012); Roderick (2012).
14 Faria et al. (2017).

A Profile of How School Support Organizations Facilitate the Use of Indicator Systems in Chicago and New York

In both Chicago and New York, intermediary organizations have helped support indicator use by providing data analytic capacity and outside facilitation.[A] In these districts, the use of EWIs around dropout prevention has led to considerable improvements in graduation rates over the last 10 years.[B] This box illustrates the potential roles for indicator systems by describing the work and challenges from the perspectives of two people who have been working with schools around indicator use from the Network for College Success (NCS) in Chicago and New Visions for Public Schools (New Visions) in New York—Eliza Moeller, the Associate Director for Research and Data Strategy at NCS, and Susan Fairchild, formerly Director of Program Analysis and Applied Research at New Visions.

Helping Schools Identify and Support Students

A central component of indicator systems is the work of identifying struggling students based on data and providing targeted interventions to meet their needs. It can be daunting to organize student-level data into indicator reports that are easy to use in practice. In New York, Fairchild described how district data systems can produce tens of thousands of data points over the course of a single day; the volume of information and the challenge of interpreting and acting on it all can be overwhelming. The data must be organized in a way that makes it easy to use in practice, and New Visions helps practitioners sort through the volume of data.

Even when the data are organized into useful reports, Moeller and Fairchild noted that teachers and school staff frequently require support around how to act on the information. Both organizations use protocol-driven conversations among teacher teams and administrators around student-level data. These include protocols for case-managing data on individual students, as well as data analysis for supporting schools' decision-making at critical junctures, for instance in the programming of students' course schedules and monitoring of their progress toward graduation. Examples of these materials in Chicago can be found online through the NCS Freshman OnTrack Toolkit.[C]

Facilitating the Use of Setting-Level Data for School Improvement

As educators use EWIs to identify students who need support and develop strategies to help them, they often recognize a need to change school structures to better support groups of students at a time. NCS and New Visions help schools use setting-level data to provide feedback to staff on the efficacy of their intervention approaches and strategies. They try to do this largely in real time, or at least with sufficient time to make adjustments to school strategies based on initial assessments of effects.

NCS works with data analysts to develop tailored data reports for schools out of the data systems run by the district. Their staff work with school teams *"to figure out...what the problem of practice is, figure out the data you think people need, and [then] to build the report,"* Moeller explained. No one at the school level has to *"put the variables together,"* or build the graph. The data tools that NCS develops and provides to schools are intended *"to bridge some space between the data that's available to schools' on the [district] systems,"* on the one hand, and the data *"in the format that is helpful for schools"* on the other. Often, this work involves developing tools that scrape data available to schools on the district dashboard, and, as Moeller put it, turn that data *"into the graph that you want to use at your grade level team meeting."*

Moeller discussed the need to go beyond focusing on individual students in an indicator system to analyzing setting level data. School personnel need to analyze data on themselves—on how they're organized and how the school operates as an organization. To do this, they use data-informed protocols that link student performance to school structures, and even individual teachers and classrooms. That often requires asking difficult, sometimes intrusive questions about teachers' classrooms. For example, setting-level data might show that failure rates are higher in English classes than in math classes. Reflecting on why these differences exist can lead to improvements in instructional practices so that more students have a successful experience in English, but that reflection requires

---

A   Fairchild et al. (2013); Pitcher et al. (2016).

B   Chicago reports increases in its five-year graduation rates from 57 percent in 2011 to 78 percent in 2017, available at: **http://www.cps.edu/SchoolData/Pages/SchoolData.aspx** New York reports increases in graduation rates from 61 percent in the 2004 ninth-grade cohort (2008 graduates)

to 73 percent in the 2012 ninth-grade cohort (2017 graduates), available at: **http://schools.nyc.gov/Accountability/data/GraduationDropoutReports/default.htm**

C   For more information, visit **https://ncs.uchicago.edu/freshman-on-track-toolkit**

teachers to question what they are doing and be willing to try out different strategies. An outside organization can play a key role in supporting change since they can structure the conversation in ways that are not as threatening as they would be if led by school leadership or by peers in other departments.

Likewise, at New Visions, Fairchild pointed out that indicators allow educators to identify patterns or trends in the data that can lead to an important conversation about what's going on and why. Yet, while a pattern or trend may be evident, understanding its origin and then selecting a solution to address the underlying problem, as well as a strategy for evaluating the effectiveness of that solution over time, is a complex and uncertain process. In those conversations, which both Moeller and Fairchild described supporting in various ways, indicators help teachers and school staff make explicit their own assumptions about students and what drives student performance. In articulating those narratives, they open up a space for interrogating those beliefs—for treating them, as Fairchild explained, as testable hypotheses. They use data to illuminate the intersections between student performance and school practices. *"If we're not tracking whether or not [an intervention] is actually happening,"* Fairchild observed, *"we don't know whether or not the intervention is working."*

At both NCS and New Visions, indicators play a key role in school improvement effort and professional development. *"People are so wedded to their narratives"* about what's going on in their buildings and why, Fairchild explained, that it becomes a form of what she referred to as *"cultural entrapment."* Indicators become a key means, in Fairchild's words, *"of breaking down those blind spots,"* and *"squashing that myth"* that is holding your practice, your school back. Fairchild described the difficulty of the work. *"Structuring highly effective teams...[around] adult learning is the single hardest thing that I have ever had to deal with in my entire career."*

An additional role that NCS plays is to serve as a connector across schools by bringing school leadership teams together to look at each other's data. For example, seeing that students with similar backgrounds and test scores have better attendance and grades at one school than another can lead to questions about differences in practices. This can support innovation and the spread of best practices across schools, which otherwise might not occur.

Helping Bridge School Improvement Efforts with Accountability Policies

Fairchild and Moeller both note that the work of supporting schools in making use of indicators in practice to meet district accountability goals is delicate work, but immensely powerful. The metrics included in accountability scores send a signal to schools about district priorities, but school practitioners need to develop strategies for improving their metrics. Indicator data can help school practitioners reach long-term summative goals that are emphasized in accountability policies, if they have school-level systems with real-time indicator data that are highly predictive of those long-term goals.[D] Well-designed indicator systems can provide the means for schools to continually evaluate how they are doing in meeting their goals throughout the year, rather than simply waiting until the end of the year to see how they did. The work of school support organizations like NCS and New Visions complements many district-level functions by facilitating the organization and discussion of processing data that help them reach the summative goals.

Both Fairchild and Moeller pointed out that with the right supports, indicator systems can provide schools with a valuable perspective on their own work, a perspective that can be lacking in district-driven accountability systems. New Visions, Fairchild argued, places an emphasis on value of thinking about *"data use as a way of holding onto the long view"* in the context of accountability systems. Similarly, Moeller pointed out that focusing on the year-to-year changes in metrics included on district accountability scorecards can seem random, but helping schools examine trends over time and patterns in the data can provide an entry point for contextualizing a school's performance on a district accountability system in a way that provides meaningful opportunities for learning.

D Weiss (2012).

CHAPTER 2

Which Indicators Should be the Focus of the System?

Districts across the country are currently tracking a large array of indicators that they believe matter for students' long-term educational attainment. The number of data points that some school administrators receive on their students can be overwhelming and make it difficult to set priorities for improvement efforts. The indicators that they use may be chosen for different reasons, and serve different purposes. It is not always clear which indicators hold the most potential for improving students' outcomes. There is a need for broader knowledge about what *is* an effective indicator. Just as importantly, school practitioners need to know: what is *not* an effective indicator?

The decision of which indicators to focus on should be shaped by the plan for how the indicators will be used; indicators are not effective if practitioners do not have strategies to act on them. Some indicators may be difficult to calculate in a timely way, or may be confusing and difficult to use. If efforts are to be sustained, it is important that school staff see some pay-off in student outcomes for the considerable amount of time it takes to monitor, develop strategies, and work to improve indicators.[15] Besides knowing whether an indicator is predictive, we really need to know: what *is* an effective indicator *in practice,* and what is *not* an effective indicator *in practice?*

Ideal Properties of Indicators

Ideally, indicators display the following properties, with each building on the prior:

- **Predictiveness:** An indicator must show a strong relationship to eventual diploma/degree completion to be useful as an indicator. A strongly-predictive indicator allows practitioners to be sure that students identified as at-risk of not attaining a diploma/

degree really do need intervention. When practitioners use indicators that are not strongly predictive of educational attainment, they risk missing students who need support, wasting limited resources, and mis-estimating the effects of their practices on students' educational attainment.[16]

- **Usability and Clarity:** Indicators that are easy to gather and to understand are more likely to be used than complex indicators that are not well-understood or difficult to construct. Likewise, indicator systems that focus attention on a small number of indicators allow for more targeted approaches than systems that contain many different indicators. To the extent that indicator systems contain many data elements, there is the risk that practitioners will focus on those elements that are easiest to track and manipulate, even if they have less potential leverage than others for improving educational attainment than other indicators in the system. At the same time, educators may benefit from multiple indicators if they provide complementary types of information that can aid in intervention efforts.[17]

- **Real-Time/Right-Time Availability:** Indicators that are available in "real-time" or on a periodic basis at the "right time" (e.g., by school quarter or semester) can be used for continuous improvement, providing information about whether strategies that school staff are using to support students are working. This allows practitioners to change course, make adjustments, or double down own what they are doing at multiple time points during the school year. When indicators are only available annually, it takes an entire year to know whether the strategies had any effect, and students will have already moved on to the next grade level.[18]

---

15 For example, Davis et al. (2013) describe the frustration that occurs when teachers meet regularly on student data, yet see no progress.
16 Gleason & Dynarski (2002); Bowers, Sprott, & Taff (2013).
17 Balfanz & Byrnes (2006); Bowers et al. (2013).
18 See Davis et al. (2013) for a description of teacher team meetings that use real time data.

- **Direct causal linkage to educational attainment:** Indicators that directly affect students' educational attainment can not only be used to ascertain a student's level of risk or readiness, but also can be used as proximal outcomes to target changes in school practice. Some indicators might predict educational attainment, but not actually lead to improved outcomes if they were to change because they are only spuriously related to attainment (i.e., some third factor influences both the indicator and educational attainment).

- **Malleability:** Indicators that are causally linked to educational attainment can be targeted for improving students' attainment, but if educators cannot change them, or do not know how to change them, then they may not be useful as key components of the indicator system. Indicators that are known to be malleable through specific practices—and that are strongly and causally linked to educational attainment—provide the greatest opportunity for improving students' outcomes.

The indicators in use by schools and school districts across the country vary considerably on these dimensions, including the strength of their predictiveness of educational attainment. There is a need for a guide that discerns the quality of different indicators along these dimensions. However, at this point, there is insufficient research to evaluate any of the indicators being used along all of these dimensions. The following section describes the research that currently exists, and Chapter 3 discusses research that is needed on indicators to move the field of indicator work further.

What are Effective Indicators of High School and College Readiness?

There are a wide array of indicators that have been proposed for early intervention around high school graduation and college readiness. For example, Bowers, Sprott, and Taff (2013) identified 110 predictors of high school dropout/graduation that had been used in the literature, including course failures, low grades, disciplinary problems, grade retention, low standardized test scores, and

many more. Based on an extensive review of literature, Gurantz and Borsato (2012) suggested a menu of college-readiness indicators that included academic indicators (e.g., students' GPA, failures, course completion in science and math, maintaining achievement level across school transition years, performance on benchmark and college entrance exams, participation in college-prep coursework), indicators of tenacity (e.g., attendance, disciplinary infractions, mastery orientation, and self-discipline), and indicators for college knowledge (e.g., understanding of application processes and financial aid, completion of college applications, meeting with college advisor, having a post-graduation plan, independent study skills, participation in the SAT/ACT).[19]

Because the list of potential indicators is long, this section provides an overview of the existing research to provide guidance as to which indicators are most likely to have leverage for improving educational attainment. Especially in the area of high school graduation, there is now a general consensus around the general types of indicators that form the core of the indicator system. The specific calculation method of the indicators, and how they are used, are less consistently agreed upon. Research on indicators of college readiness suggests a great deal of similarity with indicators of high school graduation, but there are considerably more questions about how complex a college readiness indicator system should be.

Most high school graduation indicator systems focus on students' grades, attendance, and behavior. These are characterized in some places as the "ABCs" (attendance, behavior, course performance), and others as "BAG" (behavior, attendance, and grades). At the middle grades level, systems are largely based on research in Philadelphia which discerned indicators in the middle grade years that predicted students with a high likelihood of dropping out of high school, based on grades, attendance, and behavior.[20] At the high school level, early warning systems largely focus on ninth-grade course failures and attendance, based on research in Chicago showing both are highly predictive of eventually graduating.[21] Studies in many other places (e.g.,

---

19 See Gurantz & Borsato (2012) and Bowers et al. (2013) for lists of college readiness and graduation indicators that are in use.
20 Neild et al. (2007); Neild & Balfanz (2006).

21 Allensworth & Easton (2005; 2007)

Predictive analytics is an approach that is growing in popularity to estimate an individual's likelihood of attaining an outcome, such as high school graduation, with a large quantity of data, to better target interventions.[E] It utilizes machine learning to extract information from large-scale databases and, in some cases, uses different statistical models to optimize results. This produces the most accurate prediction of the outcome, based on the data available. For this reason, predictive analytics is considered a promising approach for extracting information from the large quantity of data. At the same time, while the indica-

tors produced can be highly predictive, the approach has some disadvantages, including:

- Lack of transparency of how the estimates of an individual student's likelihood of attaining an outcome are created, making it difficult for practitioners to know what supports are needed.

- Replicating and reinforcing previous inequitable or discriminatory patterns because models are based on historical data.

- A focus on individual student intervention when setting level strategies may be more appropriate.

E   For more information, see Burke et al. (2017) and Porter & Balu (2017).

Baltimore, California, New York, Ohio, and Texas) have also consistently found that students' course grades (e.g., GPAs, course passing) and student attendance in the middle grades and high school are very strong predictors of eventually graduating high school.[22]

In Chicago, for example, students' ninth-grade GPAs were found to predict high school graduation with 80 percent accuracy.[23] In contrast, students' eighth-grade test scores and background characteristics (e.g., race, economic status, gender, age when entered high school, prior mobility) together only predicted graduates with 65 percent accuracy. Using all of the information on test scores and backgrounds together with grades, only increased the accuracy of the prediction to 81 percent— barely any better than just using GPAs alone. In a study of middle grade predictors of high school success in Chicago, the combination of indicators of grades and attendance provided the best prediction of high school on-track rates, and additional information—including test scores and measures of student "grit"—did not further improve the prediction and thus are not necessary components of an indicator system.[24]

More research is needed on the use of behavior data in indicator systems. While the evidence around grades and attendance is strong, there is less consistency about the predictive strength of behavior data. A number of studies find that data on students' behavior (e.g., suspensions, behavior marks) are strongly predictive of high school graduation.[25] Yet, behavior was not found to be predictive in Chicago, above and beyond grades and attendance.[26] It could be that differences in how behavioral data is collected in different places, or differences in behavioral expectations, discipline policies, or interventions for disciplinary infractions across different places, cause behavior data to be stronger predictors of dropout in some places than in others. Or, it could be that the different methodologies that have been used to study indicators result in different conclusions.

There is also a challenge in using behavior data as an EWI in practice. One issue stems from the ambiguity in how to define behavior indicators; different definitions could flag different students, and there is not a consensus on the best ways to construct these indicators. This stems, in part, from the different ways in which behavior

---

22 Studies find that grades and attendance in grades prior to tenth grade are predictive of high school graduation, or a milestones strongly associated with graduation, such as passing an exit exam or being on-track to graduate in eleventh grade, include: Bowers et al. (2013); Allensworth, Gwynne, Moore, & de la Torre (2014); Balfanz & Byrnes (2006); Balfanz, Byrnes, & Fox (2015); Hartman, Wilkins, Gregory, Gould, & D'Souza (2011); Hess, Lyons, Corsino, & Wells (1989); Norbury, Wong, Wan, Reese, Dhillon, & Gerdeman (2012); Rumberger

(1995); Stuit et al. (2016); Balfanz, Herzog, & MacIver (2007); Zau & Betts (2008); Neild & Balfanz (2006); Bowers (2010); Kurlaender, Reardon, & Jackson (2008); Kieffer & Marinell (2012); BERC (2011).

23 Allensworth (2013).

24 Allensworth et al. (2014).

25 Balfanz & Byrnes (2006); Bowers et al. (2013); Lehr, Sinclair, & Christenson (2004); Davis et al. (2013).

26 Allensworth et al. (2014).

Which Data Elements Make the Most Predictive Indicators?

High School Graduation EWIs

- Course Grades/Failures
- Attendance

College Readiness Indicators

- Course Grades (GPA)

What Are Other Potentially Predictive Indicators?

High School Graduation EWIs

- **Behavior Indicators**: depend on the school or district
- **Test Scores**: in places with graduation exams

College Readiness Indicators

- **Coursework**: research base is not sufficient
- **Learning Skills and College Knowledge**: research base is not sufficient, and may depend on college context
- **Test Scores**: predict college access, but not college performance
- **Completion of Milestones**: such as FAFSA, and college applications

---

data is collected and how schools and individual practitioners define and interpret behaviors. Disproportionate disciplinary actions for male students and students of color also could impact how to interpret discipline data as a predictor and the appropriate level for intervention. Another issue comes from the tendency for teachers to focus on indicators of behavior to the exclusion of other indicators when using a system with multiple indicators that include student behavior.[27] Student behavior problems are such a pressing concern that they can dominate educators' attention and goals. At the same time, there is evidence that a school suspension can be the first step of a downward spiral for students' academic achievement.[28] Schools might choose to incorporate behavioral indicators in their indicator systems so as not to overlook students who have not yet shown other signs of struggle.

Test scores are much weaker predictors of high school graduation than grades and attendance. Test scores are often included in indicator systems to identify students who may struggle academically. However, test scores do not improve the prediction of high school graduation above grades and attendance. Incorporating indicators that do not help practitioners better identify students who need support increases the complexity of the indicator system without necessarily doing a better job of identifying specific students. This can distract educators' attention from students who need support to those who do not.

At the same time, there are reasons practitioners may want to include test scores in an indicator system. One purpose would be as contextual information, to help practitioners figure out why a student might be struggling. For example, if a student with a high standardized math test scores struggles in her math class, it suggests that the issue may be due to factors other than academic difficulty, which might point to a specific type of intervention.

In several states, students are required to pass standardized tests to graduate (e.g., New York Regents Exam, Massachusetts Comprehensive Assessment System), including a few states that use the two Common Core State Standards Assessments, Partnership for Assessment of Readiness for College and Careers (PARCC), and Smarter Balanced Assessment Consortium (SBAC) as a graduation requirement (e.g., New Mexico, Washington). In these cases, tests have a direct link to attainment and may be important indicators to include in an early warning system.

Finally, the dominance of standardized tests in school accountability makes students' test performance a priority in most high schools, and incorporation of indicators based on tests could provide coherence for school improvement efforts. However, because testing plays such a prominent role in school accountability systems, care should be taken so that information on testing does not dominate practitioners' efforts to the exclusion of other indicators that are more predictive of educational attainment.

---

27 Davis et al. (2013).
28 Balfanz et al. (2015).

College readiness indicator systems tend to incorporate a wider array of indicators than systems for high school graduation. Success in higher education generally requires more than academic preparation; this has led to the development of potentially very complex college readiness indicator systems. For example, Conley (2012) developed the Four Keys to College and Career Readiness model to describe the skills and knowledge needed for success in credit-bearing general education courses or a two-year certificate program: key cognitive strategies, key content knowledge, key learning skills and techniques, and key transition knowledge and skills.[29] Another framework, the College Readiness Indicator System, includes indicators in three areas: Academic preparedness—such as GPA, coursework, test scores; college knowledge—such as understanding of admissions and financial aid processes and filling out applications; and academic tenacity—including attendance, disciplinary infractions, mastery orientation and self-discipline.[30] The addition of skills and knowledge beyond the academic in both models stems from the more complex nature of college, which relies on students applying and enrolling in college, navigating complex systems around financial aid, and attending very different types of postsecondary programs and institutions.

Indicators based on students' course grades are the strongest predictors of college graduation. Studies that use unweighted high school GPAs from students' transcripts as a potential indicator of college performance and graduation tend to find that they are the strongest predictors of college grades and of college graduation, compared to other potential academic indicators, such as test scores.[31] One of the most rigorous studies to-date, which used extensive data on 21 flagship universities from across the country, as well as public universities in four states, found that each standard deviation increase in GPA was associated with an increase of 6 to 10 percentage points in the likelihood of graduation, depending on the selectivity of the college. This compared to less than a 2 percentage point increase in the likelihood of graduation for a standard deviation increase in SAT or ACT scores.[32] Several studies suggest that the threshold of 3.0 high school GPA is the point at which students' probability of graduating college becomes greater than 50 percent, among those students who enroll in a four-year college.[33] In Chicago, this has led to an practice of aiming for "Bs or better" in developing goals for students in both the middle grades and high school, and an indicator of 3.0 as an indicator to track for measuring goals toward college readiness.[34]

One concern about using grades in indicator systems is that it is not clear to educators why grades are more powerful indicators of future success than test scores and coursework, which are more traditional indicators of academic preparation for college. For practitioners who are used to setting goals around students' attainment of specific skills as measured on tests, setting goals around students' grades can seem counter-intuitive and counterproductive. Often, there is concern among practitioners that focusing school goals on improving grades, attendance, and behavior will result in lowering standards or diverting attention away from efforts to students' academic skills and content knowledge. Furthermore, local and national policies often emphasize metrics based on standardized tests in accountability policies, ensuring that practitioners' primary efforts are focused on improving students' content knowledge and academic skills as measured by tests. In practice, test score gains are higher among students who attend class more often and earn higher grades; both represent students' engagement in class.[35] Thus, efforts to improve students' grades and attendance can also have benefits for their test scores.

29 Conley (2012).
30 Borsato et al. (2013).
31 Bowen, Chingos, & McPherson (2009); Camara & Echternacht (2000); Geiser & Santelices (2007); Geiser & Studley (2002); Roderick, Nagaoka, & Allensworth (2006); Allensworth & Clark (2018).
32 Bowen et al. (2009).
33 Roderick et al. (2006); Bowen et al. (2009).

34 NCS has been conducting performance management sessions for Chicago public high school leaders support their efforts to help more students earn a 3.0 or higher as a benchmark for college readiness since 2013-14. The sessions were intended to help schools use their own data and ideas from peers to create actionable plans to improve the readiness level of students for college.
35 Allensworth, Correa, & Ponisciak (2008); Allensworth & Luppescu (2018).

Another concern that arises when using grades as indicators of college readiness is that they may not represent equivalent levels of achievement across high schools. The fact that GPAs are so predictive of college outcomes suggests that the variability that exists across schools must be small relative to the signaling power of GPAs as indicators of readiness. We find this to be the case, looking at data in Chicago. While GPAs do not represent exactly the same levels of academic skills and behaviors across schools, the differences in GPAs across schools for students with the same test scores and attendance are less than 0.5 a GPA point at extremely different high schools, and only about 0.2 points at more comparable high schools. There are only very small differences in GPAs by high school once we compare students taking similar classes under similar conditions with the same attendance and test scores.[36]

Bowen, Chingos, and McPherson (2009) also reached the conclusion that the differences across high schools in GPAs as a signal for college readiness was small, relative to the signal they provide, using data from their national sample of colleges.

Test scores are widely used as college-readiness indicators; they primarily matter for college admissions, not for performance in college. Almost all college readiness indicator systems incorporate test scores as a primary indicator, and sometimes their only indicator, including college entrance exam scores—the ACT and the SAT, common core assessments (the PARCC and Smarter Balanced Assessments), and other state accountability tests. This is consistent with their state-level accountability systems; all states use standardized tests to judge students' progress toward college readiness goals, with 45 states using college entrance exams (ACT or SAT scores).[37] *The What Works Clearinghouse Practice Guide* on how to prepare students for college repeatedly suggests using standardized assessments to gauge student readiness for college.[38]

A search of the literature on college readiness suggests that students' standardized test scores (e.g., ACT and SAT scores) are strong predictors of college graduation, with some studies suggesting they are similar in predictiveness to high school GPA. However, most of these studies have been conducted in collaboration with testing companies, and use student-reported GPAs in their comparisons.[39] Student-reported GPAs are more weakly correlated with college outcomes than GPAs taken from transcripts,[40] so these studies tend to underestimate the predictive power of high school grades and over-estimate the contribution of test scores.[41] The studies that find standardized test scores to be predictive of college outcomes often do not control for potential spurious factors, such as student background characteristics, the types of colleges in which students enroll, or the characteristics of students' high schools (e.g., mean socioeconomic status). Studies that do control for these factors—comparing students in the same colleges, or controlling for high school characteristics—find that the tests have very modest predictive power when comparing similar students at similar schools.[42] Among students in similar types of colleges, who come from similar high schools, ACT and SAT scores have weak-to-no associations with college graduation. In contrast, high school GPAs remain highly predictive among students in the same colleges, compared to others from their high school or similar high schools. When predicting which students are *ready to succeed* in college, once they have enrolled, indicators based on grades are far superior to those based on test scores.

While students' ACT/SAT scores and their coursework are not strongly predictive of college graduation, they do add predictive power beyond GPAs in predicting college *enrollment*. ACT and SAT scores are often used in college admissions decisions, and this makes them meaningful for college outcomes. For predicting whether students are admitted to college, test scores

36 Allensworth & Clark (2018); Allensworth & Luppescu (2018).
37 Nayar (2015).
38 Tierney, Bialey, Constantine, Finkelstein, & Hurd (2009).
39 For example, Camara & Echternaucht (2000); Kobrin, Patterson, Shaw, Mattern, & Barbuti (2008); Noble & Sawyer (2002).
40 Kuncel, Credé, & Thomas (2005); Zwick & Himmelfarb (2011).
41 Another study that has been cited as showing that tests have a similar relationship with college graduation as GPA

uses weighted GPA rather than unweighted GPA. Weighted GPAs combine information on which courses students took (e.g., Honors and AP courses that get weighted more highly) with the grades students received. Coursework has not been shown to be predictive of college graduation in studies that control for students' GPAs.
42 Allensworth & Clark (2018); Rothstein (2004); Bowen et al. (2009); Hiss & Franks (2014).

are almost as predictive as GPAs, and provide additional information beyond GPAs alone.[43] Higher standardized test scores also help students get into more selective colleges. This can have an indirect influence on college graduation, since students are more likely to graduate at colleges that tend to be more selective, compared to students with similar qualifications who attend less selective schools.[44]

Thus, higher test scores and stronger coursework make it more likely that students will get into colleges where more students graduate, even if they do not result in better outcomes compared to other students at the same college. This nuance makes it tricky to decide to what degree test scores should be included as primary indicators in a college readiness system. While they matter for college enrollment, their ultimate influence on college degree attainment is small, and mediated by college choice. If the focus of the college readiness system is on these indicators, rather than on students' GPA, the system may end up having little influence on college degree *attainment*. There is a need for research on the trade-offs that come from including students' test scores as a primary indicator in a college readiness indicator system.

Participation in advanced coursetaking is only sometimes linked by research to greater college success. College readiness efforts often include efforts to expand advanced coursetaking, particularly courses that provide opportunities for college credit in high school such as Advanced Placement (AP). Districts and schools often use coursetaking as an indicator of college readiness. Advanced coursework serves as a signal to colleges when making admissions decisions; this makes it a predictor of college enrollment. However, its prediction of college completion is less studied than grades or test scores, and the evidence about the influence of coursework is mixed.

AP is used across the country to provide opportunities for advanced coursetaking and college credit for high scores on an exam. However, in most studies that control for demographics and prior characteristics—comparing students

with similar backgrounds—researchers find students who took AP courses in high school perform no better on college freshman GPA, persistence, and completion than comparison students.[45] One study did find positive effects for providing teacher training and payments to eleventh- and twelfth-grade students and their teachers for passing AP exams; students in participating schools increased their AP passing rates, college retention, and wages.[46]

Other forms of advanced coursework have been studied less than AP courses. One study of the International Baccalaureate Programme (IB) found that IB students were significantly more likely to persist in college after two years.[47] Dual enrollment, the opportunity for students to take college courses for college credit while still enrolled in high school, has shown promise; studies have found students who participate in dual enrollment programs are more likely to persist and complete college.[48] Thus, there is a basis for including at least some types of coursework into college readiness indicator systems. However, more research is needed to know how much emphasis there should be on these indicators.

The college enrollment process includes specific tasks that can be indicators. As a part of supporting enrollment in college and the college choice process, some high schools use data systems to track students' progress on critical milestones that draw on college knowledge, such as whether and where students submitted college applications and completed the FAFSA. These systems enable counselors and other school staff to monitor the progress of students in the college application process and provide more targeted guidance. Next to high school GPAs, the factor that most strongly predicts whether students will succeed in college is the institution at which they enroll, particularly the institutional graduation rate. This makes the role that high schools play in supporting students' college choices particularly important. Thus, using data systems to support students in the college application and choice process helps position students to attain a college degree.

---

43 Easton, Johnson, & Sartain (2017); Kelley-Kemple, Proger, & Roderick (2011, September 9).
44 Coca (2014); Roderick et al. (2006).
45 Dougherty, Mellor, & Jian (2006); Geiser & Santelices (2004); Klopfenstein (2004); Sadler & Sonnert (2010).
46 Jackson (2014).
47 Coca et al. (2012).
48 An (2013); Karp (2011).

Academic readiness for college may differ by major and post-secondary institution, especially in the area of college knowledge. One complication that occurs in studying college readiness indicators is that colleges vary greatly in their admissions standards and the factors that matter for success, both by institution and by major within an institution. The academic qualifications that are needed to be admitted to different types of colleges vary considerably, and level of academic preparedness that students need to succeed at one college, or in one type of major, may be very different from another college or a different major.

This makes the definition of "ready for college" contingent on the admissions standards of different institutions and what is required to complete a degree, as well as the characteristics of the institution (e.g., size, financial aid packages). It is further complicated by the fact that schools with the most selective admissions criteria also tend to have the largest capacity to provide financial and academic supports to students who are struggling. Thus, the colleges that expect the most of their students in terms of academic skills, study skills, and tenacity also might be providing students with the most support in those areas. In the end, students might need stronger academic preparation, college knowledge, and tenacity to get admitted to selective colleges, but need lower levels academic preparation, college knowledge, and tenacity to graduate if they do gain admission to those colleges. There is a need to better understand how schools should incorporate the variation in college outcomes by institution and major into their college readiness indicator systems—whether the same indicators matter, but with different thresholds, or whether they operate differently based on the type of college.

The issue of context is particularly salient when considering non-academic indicators, such as those of "college knowledge," perseverance, or study skills, which are less easily measured. Despite the prominence of these indicators in popular frameworks, there is little evidence about the degree to which they predict college degree attainment. The research base that supports their use comes from interviews of faculty members about what they think matters, or the recognition that students leave college when they encounter barriers—such as having financial holds on their records—that have the potential to be ameliorated by being better able to navigate the college environment. There is not yet research that measures students' college knowledge prior to attending college to see how it is related to eventual college completion. And it seems very likely that the influence of these factors would be moderated by the type of college and program within the college that students attend.

Further Limitations in What We Know About Specific Indicators

At the beginning of this chapter we identified five characteristics that indicators ideally have: predictiveness, usability and clarity, real-time/right-time availability, having a direct causal linkage to educational attainment, and malleability. For school practitioners considering different indicators for the focus of their work, it would be useful to have a guide to help sort through the pluses and minuses of using different potential indicators. At this point, there is no such guide. While properties such as clarity and availability are easy to discern, other properties require research, and the current research base is insufficient. Research on indicator predictiveness and malleability exists for some types of indicators, but research that allows comparisons among indicators is sparse, scattered, and difficult to access. There is little-to-no research that attempts to provide evidence of causality.

It is essential that indicators be predictive of later educational attainment if they are to lead to improvements in students' attainment. Yet, determining which indicators to include in an indicator system requires consideration of the local context and how the indicator will be used in schools. Almost all of the research on the most common indicators used in EWI systems has been based in just a few cities. There are questions about whether indicators that have been developed in other places will work the same way in other districts. There also are often questions about whether the patterns observed in the general population hold for particular subgroups of students.[49] For college readiness indicators, in particular, there is much to learn about the ways in which college-level factors interact with high school preparation.

---

[49] Two studies that examine ninth-grade on-track indicators for students with disabilities and English language learners found similar patterns as in the general population (Gwynne, Lesnick Hart, & Allensworth, 2009; Gwynne, Pareja, Ehrlich, & Allensworth, 2012), but also identified some areas of difference.

CHAPTER 3

Gaps in Knowledge and Next Steps for Research

Going forward, one of the most important tasks for the field will be to balance the promise of using indicator systems as part of a comprehensive strategy for increasing educational attainment with some of the ongoing challenges and cautions identified here. There is a growing evidence base around the indicators that matter for increasing attainment. However, there still remain a number of important challenges to effective indicator use, as described throughout this document. We see four areas of research that are of particular priority for using indicators to improve educational attainment.

Areas of Research for Using Indicators to Improve Educational Attainment

1. Teacher Beliefs, School Policies, Student Interventions, and Instructional Practices to Improve Students' Grades

Research on high school and college graduation indicators consistently shows that students' GPAs are an exceptionally strong predictor of high school and college graduation, and a much stronger predictor than test scores, coursework, or background characteristics. Grades are measures of students' effort and engagement in their classes; they tend to be based on a combination of academic skills and effort, including students' course attendance, assignment completion, and participation—all factors that also matter for college completion.[50] Efforts to increase students' educational attainment and increase equity by race and gender will need to focus on improving students' grades, perhaps through more effective student-level interventions, school-level policies, and classroom-level instructional practices.

There is a need for more research that tests teacher assumptions about grades and grading practices. While most practitioners recognize that students' grades are an important indicator of later educational attainment, many also hold contradictory beliefs about whether schools should have strategies to improve students' grades. For example, some educators believe that failure teaches students a lesson—helping them to be more resilient. They might be hesitant to work on strategies to prevent failures. Others may believe that grades should sort students, and not embrace a goal of getting all students earning As and Bs. They may also believe teachers who give too many As and Bs must not be challenging students sufficiently, and would increase their expectations or reduce support if all students were fully engaged and successful. Thus, there is a need for better understanding the belief systems that hold back schools from working on improving grades, and evidence about whether these concerns are valid, such as what happens to students' educational attainment if schools are successful at raising grades, using different types of strategies.

Educators need school-wide strategies on grades that have long-term benefits. There are many policies and practices that are currently used to improve course grades. For example some schools have enacted school-wide policies requiring teachers to enter grades in an online portal visible to parents, making grading practices clearly aligned to specific criteria, or introducing a "no zero" policy. There is not yet evidence about whether these strategies are beneficial or adverse for students' educational attainment. Practitioners sometimes worry that providing support to students whose grades are low, or who are not completing work or are missing class, will

---

50 Bowers (2009; 2011); Rosenkranz, de la Torre, Stevens, & Allensworth (2014); Farrington et al. (2012); Willingham, Pollack, & Lewis (2002).

keep students from developing skills as independent learners, making them less likely succeed in college. Thus, it is essential that practitioners know what strategies and practices for improving course grades are effective and are based in improved learning and eventually result in higher educational attainment.

There is not yet clear guidance on the implications for teachers' instructional practices. Using indicators to monitor students and reach out when they need support can lead to teachers altering the ways in which they engage with students. Besides setting criteria for grades and then determining whether students meet those criteria, school goals around improving grades can lead teachers to make sure students have the supports they need to be able to meet the criteria they set. Yet, practitioners and policymakers often worry that goals around improving students' grades will lead to inflating grades, resulting in less learning and lower standards, or giving students a false sense of their academic skills. Thus,

teachers need guidance about how to support students in ways that maintain high standards.

Besides reaching out to students who fall behind, it may be possible for teachers to improve students' grades by altering their instruction in ways that promote strong student engagement. Grades assess student effort (e.g., attendance, study habits), assignment completion, class participation, time management, help-seeking behavior, metacognitive strategies, and social skills, in addition to assessing students' content knowledge and academic skills. The array of factors that are not measured by tests, but captured by grades, have been described as non-cognitive skills, 21st Century Skills, and School Success Factors, and they seem to matter considerably for educational attainment.[51] Improving course grades could entail better attention to these factors.[52] There is a need for research that can help teachers develop and implement instructional strategies that incorporate research on the ways in which noncognitive factors influence student engagement and improve course performance.

Practitioners Need Strategies for Improving Grades that Are Meaningful for Students' Later Outcomes.

- What are teacher beliefs about grades and grading practices and how do they shape their instructional practices?
- What are the setting-level (whole school) policies that are being attempted to improve students' grades, and how effective are they?

- What are the student-level interventions that are being attempted, and how effective are they?
- What are the classroom-level instructional strategies, particularly around noncognitive/ 21st Century skills, that are being attempted, and how effective are they?

---

51 Bowers (2011); Brookhart (1991); Cross & Frary (1999); Farrington et al. (2012); Kelly (2008); Willingham et al. (2002).
52 See Farrington et al. (2012).

2. The Role of College Knowledge and Institutional Context in Defining College Readiness

High schools play a critical role in ensuring that their students are prepared and positioned for academic success in college. A substantial limitation in the research on college readiness indicators is that almost all of the studies to-date have focused only on indicators of academic preparedness, even though two of the most prominent models for college readiness indicator systems, the Four Keys and College Readiness Indicator System, both include college knowledge and skills as being key components of college readiness.[53]

There is a need to develop and validate indicators of college knowledge and skills. College knowledge and skills are included as potential indicators of college readiness because students' aspirations and participation in the financial aid, college search, and college choice processes in high school shape their eventual college outcomes.[54] The transition to college also often requires students to have the college knowledge and skills needed to navigate a new, less structured environment than the high school students attended. Students encounter new demands such as choosing courses, balancing time needed to study with other interests and responsibilities, and adapting to a social culture that may be very different from what the students have experienced. College knowledge remains poorly measured and considerably less is known about the potential predictive power of college knowledge.

It is not clear how "college readiness" depends on the post-secondary context. College graduation also is influenced by the characteristics of higher education institutions themselves, and the programs and majors into which students enroll. It is not clear what it means to be "college ready" given the myriad differences in the types of post-secondary programs and institutions that exist. What knowledge and skills students need is highly contextual; the knowledge needed to navigate a large public university differs from a small liberal arts college, a Black student attending a historically Black college will have a different social transition than if the student had enrolled in a predominately White institution, requiring different social supports and strategies. The need for college knowledge may also depend on the student herself, and the degree to which she has peer and family social capital to support her transition and navigation through college.

Colleges and programs and majors within colleges also vary in the academic readiness they require. Colleges can also develop supports and systems to help students more effectively make the transition to college, such that the degree to which students need knowledge about navigating the college process may depend on the institution they attend. As a result, there is a great deal still to be learned about how to design college readiness indicator systems in a way that captures all of this complexity.

Practitioners and Policymakers Need Greater Clarity on What It Means to Be College Ready and How That May Differ By Higher Education Institution Characteristics.

- How should college knowledge and skills be measured and how predictive are college knowledge indicators of college attainment?
- How do the college knowledge and skills needed to navigate colleges vary by institutional characteristics?

- How does the academic readiness needed to succeed academically vary by institutional characteristics and major?

---

53 Borsato et al. (2013); Conley (2007; 2012); Gurantz & Borsato (2012).

54 Avery & Kane (2004); Conley (2005); DesJardins, Ahlburg, & McCall (2006); Goodman, Hurwitz, & Smith (2015); Hoxby & Avery (2013); Page & Scott-Clayton (2015).

3. The Relationships of School-Level Indicators of School Climate with Educational Attainment and Achievement

At the school level, indicators can be used to create and sustain a framework for ongoing school improvement. Aggregations of student-level indicators provide a means for monitoring progress toward school goals around students' achievement and educational attainment. Indicators of school climate provide a big-picture perspective of the larger organizational context that influences the ability of students and teachers to be effective. Yet, there are many unanswered questions about how measures from the surveys of school organization and climate are related to improvement over time, and in different contexts, and how they should be used together with indicators of student achievement.

There is a need for more research on the relationship of school climate measures to indicators of educational attainment. Research suggests that school climate holds considerable potential for improving students' educational outcomes. Surveys are able to provide a nuanced picture of a school organization, and the ways in which teachers and students are experiencing their work. A number of studies have shown that student and teacher reports about the conditions in their schools are predictive of later outcomes.[55] However, there has not been a study that has systematically examined the relationship of school climate to the indicators of educational attain-

ment, such as attendance and grades. Studies validating the use of surveys to measure classroom instruction and school climate have predominantly focused on elementary and middle grade test scores as outcomes.

The research base on the use of surveys as tools for school improvement is very limited. One of the most widely-cited studies that validates the use of surveys as indicators of school improvement, *Organizing Schools for Improvement*, is based on survey reports from 20 years ago, only includes data from one place (Chicago), and only examines elementary schools.[56] There has been a proliferation of school climate surveys under the Every Student Succeeds Act (ESSA), which potentially provides an opportunity to examine the relationship between school context and high school and college indicators across geographic locations.[57] And there is evidence that school improvement efforts based on surveys have led to improvement in student outcomes.[58] In cities such as Chicago and New York, surveys have been continually administered for many years, allowing the opportunity to examine their use in different contexts and with different types of supports. Chicago and New York have also developed extensive student-level indicator systems over time, and we have yet to learn how schools use these different types of indicators in practice, if there is an ordering for what aspects of school climate should be worked on, or how changes in setting-level indicators lead to changes in student-level outcomes.

Practitioners Need to Better Understand How Measures of School Climate Relate to Early Warning and College Readiness Indicators.

- What is the longitudinal relationship of the survey measures of school climate with early warning and college readiness indicators?
- Is there a sequencing to how school climate measures improve?

- How do schools seeking to improve their school climate use data to strengthen their school organization and improve student achievement?

---

55 Allensworth et al. (2009); Bryk et al. (2010); Kane, Taylor, Tyler, & Wooten (2010).
56 Bryk et al. (2010).

57 Under ESSA, state accountability plans have to include four academic indicators, as well as a fifth indicator which potentially could include measures of school climate, student engagement, and other factors that could be measured by surveys.
58 Sun et al. (2017).

4. How Indicators Are Being Used to Improve Educational Attainment

The use of indicators has become a central component in school, district, and state efforts to improve students' educational attainment. It has become clear that districts and states need to do more than provide systems that include indicators that fit our criteria of being predictive, useable and clear, available at the real-time/right-time, and causally linked to attainment. The criteria of malleability won't be a reality unless schools have the knowledge and skills to interpret and act on the indicators and the time and resources to develop systems and structures for using them. Too often, schools are left on their own to develop strategies for using indicator systems and there is little evidence on what effective approaches are.

The NCS and New Visions models highlight the importance of organizing schools in ways that enable practitioners, particularly through teacher teams, to manage, interpret, and act on the information provided by indicator systems. The two models also demonstrate the essential role practitioner knowledge and skills plays in effective indicator use. However, beyond these two models, there is currently little documentation of how indicators are being used, and little-to-no systematic evidence on which approaches are effective for improving students' educational attainment, what systems and structures are needed to support these efforts, and how to develop the capacity of practitioners to use and act on indicators. There is a need to document what it is that schools are doing, particularly in those places where students' outcomes are showing considerable improvement.

Furthermore, given the important role that intermediary organizations have played in supporting the use of indicators in Chicago and New York, it would be useful to better understand how such organizations effectively support schools in the use of indicator systems, and what happens when schools do not have support. It could be that change is unlikely without an external partner, or it could be that change is simply slower without external support, or that it is not really needed and change can happen through district efforts alone. Research could identify the functions that such organizations play that are different than internal district functions. It also is not clear to what extent these organizations have been successful in Chicago and New York because they were voluntary partners to schools.

//

Practitioners Need to Know How to Effectively Use Indicator Systems.

- How are school practitioners currently using indicator systems and what are effective approaches to using indicator systems?
- What systems and structures are needed in schools and districts to effectively use indicator systems?

- How can the skills and knowledge to effectively use indicator systems be developed and what is the potential role for intermediary organizations in supporting school practitioners?
- What is the role of intermediary organizations in building the capacity of practitioners to use indicator systems?

//

Conclusion

Meeting the goals that have been set across the country to graduate all students ready for college will take extraordinary changes in schools. For decades, only about half of students graduated high school in this country, and less than a fifth of those students earned a college degree. As states, districts, and schools work to improve educational attainment, their success will likely be determined by the answers to the questions above. This is not an agenda that can be answered by researchers in one place. It will require learning across geographic contexts, across school and district conditions. And it will require researchers and practitioners learning from each other. The gains that we have started to see in districts across the country show that change is possible, even if there is still considerable work to be done, and questions to be answered, to reach the ambitious and important goals of graduating all students ready to succeed in college and career.

References

Allensworth, E.M., (2013)
The use of ninth-grade early warning indicators to improve Chicago schools. *Journal of Education for Students Placed at Risk (JESPAR), 18*(1), 68-83.

Allensworth, E.M., & Easton, J.Q. (2005)
The on-track indicator as a predictor of high school graduation. Chicago, IL: University of Chicago Consortium on Chicago School Research.

Allensworth, E.M., & Easton, J.Q. (2007)
What matters for staying on-track and graduating in Chicago Public Schools. Chicago, IL: University of Chicago Consortium on Chicago School Research.

Allensworth, E.M., & Clark, K. (2018)
Are grades an inconsistent measure of achievement across high schools? An examination of the concurrent and predictive validity of GPAs relative to standardized test scores (Working Paper). Chicago, IL: University of Chicago Consortium on School Research.

Allensworth, E.M., Correa, M., & Ponisciak, S. (2008)
From high school to the future: ACT preparation—too much, too late. Chicago, IL: University of Chicago Consortium on Chicago School Research.

Allensworth, E.M., Gwynne, J.A., Moore, P., & de la Torre, M. (2014)
Looking forward to high school and college: Middle grade indicators of readiness in Chicago Public Schools. Chicago, IL: University of Chicago Consortium on Chicago School Research.

Allensworth, E.M., & Luppescu, S. (2018)
Why do students get good grades, or bad ones? The influence of the teacher, class, school, and student (Working Paper). Chicago, IL: University of Chicago Consortium on School Research.

Allensworth, E.M., Ponisciak, S., & Mazzeo, C. (2009)
Schools teachers leave: Teacher mobility in Chicago Public Schools. Chicago, IL: University of Chicago Consortium on Chicago School Research.

An, B. (2013)
The impact of dual enrollment on college degree attainment: Do low-SES students benefit? *Educational Evaluation and Policy Analysis, 35*(1), 57-75.

Avery, C., & Kane, T.J. (2004)
Student perceptions of college opportunities: The Boston COACH Program. In C.M. Hoxby (Ed.), *College choices: The economics of where to go, when to go, and how to pay for it* (pp. 355-394). Chicago, IL: University of Chicago Press.

Balfanz, R. (2011)
Back on track to graduate. *Educational Leadership, 68*(7), 54-58.

Balfanz, R., & Byrnes, V. (2006)
Closing the mathematics achievement gap in high-poverty middle schools: Enablers and constraints. *Journal of Education for Students Placed at Risk (JESPAR), 11*(2), 143-159.

Balfanz, R., Byrnes, V., & Fox, J.H. (2015)
Sent home and put off track: The antecedents, disproportionalities, and consequences of being suspended in the 9th grade. In D.J. Losen (Ed.), *Closing the school discipline gap: Equitable remedies for excessive exclusion* (pp. 17-30). New York, NY: Teachers College Press.

Balfanz, R., Herzog, L., & MacIver, D.J. (2007)
Preventing student disengagement and keeping students on the graduation path in urban middle-grades schools: Early identification and effective interventions. *Educational Psychologist, 42*(4), 223-235.

Baltimore Education Research Consortium (BERC). (2011)
Destination graduation: Sixth-grade early warning indicators for Baltimore City Schools: Their prevalence and impact. Baltimore, MD: BERC.

Borsato, G.N., Nagaoka, J., & Foley, E. (2013)
College readiness indicator systems framework. *Voices in Urban Education, 38*, 28-35.

Bowen, W.G., Chingos, M.M., & McPherson, M.S. (2009)
Crossing the finish line: Completing college at America's public universities. Princeton, NJ: Princeton University Press.

Bowers, A.J. (2009)
Reconsidering grades as data for decision making: More than just academic knowledge. *Journal of Educational Administration, 47*(5), 609-629.

Bowers, A.J. (2010)
Grades and graduation: A longitudinal risk perspective to identify student dropouts. *The Journal of Educational Research, 103*(3), 191-207.

Bowers, A.J. (2011)
What's in a grade? The multidimensional nature of what teacher-assigned grades assess in high school. *Educational Research and Evaluation, 17*(3), 141-159.

Bowers, A.J., Sprott, R., & Taff, S.A. (2013)
Do we know who will drop out?: A review of the predictors of dropping out of high school: precision, sensitivity, and specificity. *The High School Journal, 96*(2), 77-100.

Brookhart, S.M. (1991)
Grading practices and validity. *Educational Measurement: Issues and Practice, 10*(1), 35-36.

Bruce, M., Bridgeland, J.M., Fox, J.H., & Balfanz, R. (2011)
On track for success: The use of early warning indicator and intervention systems to build a grad nation. Washington, DC: Civic Enterprises.

Bryk, A.S., Sebring, P.B., Allensworth, E.M., Luppescu, S., & Easton, J.Q. (2010)
Organizing schools for improvement: Lessons from Chicago. Chicago, IL: University of Chicago Press.

Burke, M., Parnell, A., Wesaw, A., & Kruger, K. (2017)
Predictive analysis of student data. Washington, DC: NASPA.

Camara, W.J., & Echternacht, G. (2000)
The SAT [R] I and high school grades: Utility in predicting success in college. Research Notes.

Coca, V. (2014)
New York City goes to college: A first look. New York, NY: The Research Alliance for New York City Schools.

Coca, V., Johnson, D.W., Kelley-Kemple, T., Roderick, M., Moeller, E., Williams, N., & Moragne, K. (2012)
Working to my potential: The postsecondary experiences of CPS students in the International Baccalaureate Diploma Programme. Chicago, IL: University of Chicago Consortium on Chicago School Research.

Colyvas, J.A. (2012)
Performance metrics as formal structures and through the lens of social mechanisms: When do they work and how do they influence? *American Journal of Education, 118*(2), 167-197.

Conley, D.T. (2005)
College knowledge: What it really takes for students to succeed and what we can do to get them ready. San Francisco, CA: Jossey-Bass.

Conley, D.T. (2007)
Redefining college readiness. Eugene, OR: Educational Policy Improvement Center.

Conley, D.T. (2012)
College and career ready: Helping all students succeed beyond high school. San Francisco, CA: Jossey-Bass.

Corrin, W., Sepanik, S., Rosen, R., & Shane, A. (2016)
Addressing early warning indicators: Interim impact findings from the Investing in Innovation (i3) Evaluation of Diplomas Now. New York, NY: MDRC.

Cross, L.H., & Frary, R.B. (1999)
Hodgepodge grading: Endorsed by students and teachers alike. *Applied Measurement in Education, 12*(1), 53-72.

Davis, M., Herzog, L., & Legters, N. (2013)
Organizing schools to address early warning indicators (EWIs): Common practices and challenges. *Journal of Education for Students Placed at Risk (JESPAR), 18*(1), 84-100.

DesJardins, S.L., Ahlburg, D.A., & McCall, B.P. (2006)
An integrated model of application, admission, enrollment, and financial aid. *The Journal of Higher Education, 77*(3), 381-429.

Dougherty, C., Mellor, L., & Jiang, S. (2006)
The relationship between Advanced Placement and college graduation. Austin, TX: National Center for Educational Accountability.

Easton, J.Q., Johnson, E., & Sartain, L. (2017)
The predictive power of ninth-grade GPA. Chicago, IL: University of Chicago Consortium on School Research.

Fairchild, S., Scaramellino, D., Carrino, G., Carrano, J., Gunton, B., & Donohue, B. (2013)
Navigating the data ecosystem: A case study of the adoption of a school data management system in New York City. New York, NY: New Visions for Public Schools.

Faria, A.M., Sorensen, N., Heppen, J., Bowdon, J., Taylor, S., Eisner, R., & Foster, S. (2017)
Getting students on track for graduation: Impacts of the Early Warning Intervention and Monitoring System after one year (REL 2017–272). Washington, DC: U.S. Department of Education, Institute of Education Sciences, National Center for Education Evaluation and Regional Assistance, Regional Educational Laboratory Midwest.

Farrington, C.A., Roderick, M., Allensworth, E.M., Nagaoka, J., Keyes, T.S., Johnson, D.W., & Beechum, N.O. (2012)
Teaching adolescents to become learners: The role of noncognitive factors in shaping school performance: A critical literature review. Chicago, IL: University of Chicago Consortium on Chicago School Research.

Geiser, S., & Santelices, M.V. (2007)
Validity of high-school grades in predicting student success beyond the freshman year: High-school record versus standardized tests as indicators or four-year college outcomes (Research & Occasional Paper Series: CSHE.6.07). Berkeley, CA: Center for Studies in Higher Education.

Geiser, S., & Studley, W.R. (2002)
UC and the SAT: Predictive validity and differential impact of the SAT I and SAT II at the University of California. *Educational Assessment, 8*(1), 1-26.

Gleason, P., & Dynarski, M. (2002)
Do we know whom to serve? Issues in using risk factors to identify dropouts. *Journal of Education for Students Placed at Risk (JESPAR), 7*(1), 25-41.

Goodman, J., Hurwitz, J., & Smith, J. (2015)
College Access, initial college choice and degree completion. (NBER Working Paper No. 20996). Cambridge, MA: National Bureau of Economic Research. Retrieved from http://www.nber.org/papers/w120996

Gurantz, O., & Borsato, G.N. (2012)
Building and implementing a college readiness indicator system: Lessons from the first two years of the CRIS Initiative. *Voices in Urban Education, 35*, 5-15.

Gwynne J., Lesnick, J., Hart, H., & Allensworth, E.M. (2009)
What matters for staying on-track and graduating in Chicago Public Schools: A focus on students with disabilities. Chicago, IL: University of Chicago Consortium on Chicago School Research.

Gwynne J., Pareja, A.S., Ehrlich, S.B., & Allensworth, E.M. (2012)
What matters for staying on-track and graduating in Chicago Public Schools: A focus on English language learners. Chicago, IL: University of Chicago Consortium on Chicago School Research.

Hartman, J., Wilkins, C., Gregory, L., Gould, L.F., & D'Souza, S. (2011)
Applying an on-track indicator for high school graduation: Adapting the Consortium on Chicago School Research indicator for five Texas districts (Issues & Answers Report, REL 2011–No. 100). Washington, DC: U.S. Department of Education, Institute of Education Sciences, National Center for Education Evaluation and Regional Assistance, Regional Educational Laboratory Southwest.

Hess, G.A., Jr., Lyons, A., Corsino, L., & Wells, E. (1989)
Against the odds: The early identification of dropouts. Chicago, IL: Chicago Panel on Public Policy and Finance.

Hiss, W.C., & Franks, V.W. (2014)
Defining promise: Optional standardized testing policies in American college and university admissions. Arlington, VA: The National Association for College Admission Counseling.

Hough, H., Kalogrides, D., & Loeb, S. (2017)
Using surveys of students' social-emotional skills and school climate for accountability and continuous improvement: Policy Brief 17-1. Stanford, CA: Policy Analysis for California Education.

Hoxby, C., & Avery, C. (2013)
The missing "one-offs": The hidden supply of high-achieving, low-income students. *Brookings Papers on Economic Activity, 2013*(1), 1-65.

Jackson, K.C. (2014)
Do college-prep programs improve long-term outcomes? *Economic Inquiry, 52*(1), 72-99.

Kane, T.J., McCaffrey, D.F., Miller, T., & Staiger, D.O. (2013)
Have we identified effective teachers? Validating measures of effective teaching using random assignment. Seattle, WA: Bill & Melinda Gates Foundation.

Kane, T.J., Taylor, E.S., Tyler, J.H., & Wooten, A.L. (2010)
Identifying effective classroom practices using student achievement data (NBER Working Paper No. 15803). Cambridge, MA: National Bureau of Economic Research. Retrieved from http://www.nber.org/papers/w15803

Karp, M.M. (2011)
Toward a new understanding of non-academic student support: Four mechanisms encouraging positive student outcomes in the community college (CCRC Working Paper No. 28. Assessment of Evidence Series). New York, NY: Community College Research Center, Columbia University.

Kautz, T. & Zanoni, W. (2014)
Measuring and fostering non-cognitive skills in adolescence: Evidence from Chicago Public Schools and the OneGoal Program (Unpublished manuscript). Chicago, IL: Department of Economics, University of Chicago.

Kelley-Kemple, T., Proger, A., & Roderick, M. (2011, September 9)
Engaging high school students in advanced math and science courses for success in college: Is advanced placement the answer? Presented at the fall conference of the Society for Research on Educational Effectiveness, Washington, DC.

Kelly, S. (2008)
What types of students' effort are rewarded with high marks? *Sociology of Education, 81*(1), 32-52.

Kieffer, M.J., & Marinell, W.H. (2012)
Navigating the middle grades: Evidence from New York City. New York, NY: The Research Alliance for New York City Schools.

Klopfenstein, K. (2004)
The Advanced Placement expansion of the 1990s: How did traditionally underserved students fare? *Education Policy Analysis, 12*(68), 1-15.

Kobrin, J.L., Patterson, B.F., Shaw, E.J., Mattern, K.D., & Barbuti, S.M. (2008)
Validity of the SAT® for predicting first-year college grade point average (Research Report No. 2008-5). New York, NY: College Board.

Kuncel, N.R., Credé, M., & Thomas, L.L. (2005)
The validity of self-reported grade point averages, class ranks, and test scores: A meta-analysis and review of the literature. *Review of Educational Research, 75*(1), 63-82.

Kurlaender, M., Reardon, S.F., & Jackson, J. (2008)
Middle school predictors of high school achievement in three California school districts. Santa Barbara, CA: University of California, California Dropout Research Project.

Lehr, C., Sinclair, M., & Christenson, S. (2004)
Addressing student engagement and truancy prevention during the elementary school years: A replication study of the Check & Connect Model. *Journal of Education for Students Placed at Risk (JESPAR), 9*(3), 279-301.

Li, Y., Scala, J., Gerdeman, D., & Blumenthal, D. (2016)
District guide for creating indicators for early warning systems. San Francisco, CA: REL West at WestEd.

Marsh, J.A. (2012)
Interventions promoting educators' use of data: Research insights and gaps. *Teachers College Record, 114*(11), 1-48.

Nagaoka, J., Seeskin, A., & Coca, V.M. (2017)
The educational attainment of Chicago Public Schools students: 2016. Chicago, IL: University of Chicago Consortium on School Research.

Nayar, N. (2015)
How are states reporting on college and career readiness? Washington, DC: College & Career Readiness & Success Center at the American Institutes for Research.

Neild, R., & Balfanz, R. (2006)
Unfulfilled promise: The dimensions and characteristics of Philadelphia's dropout crisis, 2000-2005. Baltimore, MD: Johns Hopkins University, Center for Social Organization of Schools.

Neild, R.C., Balfanz, R., & Herzog, L. (2007)
An early warning system. *Educational Leadership, 65*(2), 28-33.

Noble, J., & Sawyer, R. (2002)
Predicting different levels of academic success in college using high school GPA and ACT composite score. Iowa City, IA: ACT, Inc.

Noble, J.P., & Sawyer, R.L. (2004)
Is high school GPA better than admissions test scores for predicting academic success in college? *College and University, 79*(4), 17-22.

Norbury, H., Wong, M., Wan, M., Reese, K., Dhillon, S., & Gerdeman, R. (2012)
Using the freshman on-track indicator to predict graduation in two urban districts in the Midwest Region (Issues & Answers Report, REL 2012–No.134). Washington, DC: U.S. Department of Education, Institute of Education Sciences, National Center for Education Evaluation and Regional Assistance, Regional Educational Laboratory Midwest.

Page, L.C., & Scott-Clayton, J. (2015)
Improving college access in the United States: Barriers and policy responses (NBER Working Paper No. 21781). Cambridge, MA: National Bureau of Economic Research. Retrieved from http://www.nber.org/papers/w21781

Pinkus, L. (2008)
Using Early Warning Data to Improve Graduation: Rates Closing Cracks in the Education System. Washington DC: Alliance for Excellent Education

Pitcher, M.A., Duncan, S.J., Nagaoka, J., Moeller, E., Dickerson, L. & Beechum, N.O. (2016)
The Network for College Success: A capacity-building model for school improvement. Chicago, IL: Network for College Success.

Porter, K.E., & Balu, R. (2017)
Predictive modeling of K-12 academic outcomes: A primer for researchers working with education data. New York, NY: MDRC.

Roderick, M. (2012)
Drowning in data but thirsty for analysis. *Teachers College Record, 114*(11), 110309.

Roderick, M., Kelley-Kemple, T., Johnson, D.W., & Beechum, N.O. (2014)
Preventable failure: improvements in long-term outcomes when high schools focused on the ninth grade year. Chicago, IL: University of Chicago Consortium on Chicago School Research.

Roderick M., Nagaoka, J., & Allensworth, E.M. (2006)
From high school to the future: A first look at Chicago public school graduates' college enrollment, college preparation, and graduation from four-year colleges. Chicago, IL: University of Chicago Consortium on Chicago School Research.

Rosenkranz, T., de la Torre, M., Stevens, W.D., & Allensworth, E.M. (2014).
Free to fail or on-track to college: Why grades drop when students enter high school and what adults can do about it. Chicago, IL: University of Chicago Consortium on Chicago School Research.

Rothstein, J.M. (2004)
College performance predictions and the SAT. J*ournal of Econometrics, 121*(1), 297-317.

Rumberger, R. (1995)
Dropping out of middle school: A multilevel analysis of students and schools. *American Educational Research Journal, 32*(3), 583-625.

Sadler, P.M., & Sonnert, G. (2010)
High school Advanced Placement and success in college coursework in the sciences. In P.M. Sadler, G. Sonnert, R.H. Tai, & K. Klopfenstein (Eds.), *AP: A critical examination of the Advanced Placement Program* (pp. 119-137). Cambridge, MA: Harvard Education Press.

Stuit, D., O'Cummings, M., Norbury, H., Heppen, J., Dhillon, S., Lindsay, J., & Zhu, B. (2016)
Identifying early warning indicators in three Ohio school districts (REL 2016–118). Washington, DC: U.S. Department of Education, Institute of Education Sciences, National Center for Education Evaluation and Regional Assistance, Regional Educational Laboratory Midwest.

Sun, M., Penner, E.K., & Loeb, S. (2017)
Resource-and approach-driven multidimensional change: Three-year effects of school improvement grants. *American Educational Research Journal, 54*(4), 607-643.

Tierney, W.G., Bailey, T., Constantine, J., Finkelstein, N., & Hurd, N.F. (2009)
Helping students navigate the path to college: What high schools can do: A practice guide (NCEE #2009-4066). Washington, DC: National Center for Education Evaluation and Regional Assistance, Institute of Education Sciences, U.S. Department of Education.

Turner, E.O., & Coburn, C.E. (2012)
Interventions to promote data use: An introduction. *Teachers College Record, 114*(11), 1–13.

Weiss, J.A. (2012)
Data for improvement, data for accountability. *Teachers College Record, 114*(11), 1-7.

Willingham, W.W., Pollack, J.M., & Lewis, C. (2002)
Grades and test scores: Accounting for observed differences. *Journal of Educational Measurement, 39*(1), 1-37.

Zau, A., & Betts, J.R. (2008)
Predicting success, preventing failure: An investigation of the California high school exit exam. San Francisco, CA: Public Policy Institute of California.

Zwick, R., & Himelfarb, I. (2011)
The effect of high school socioeconomic status on the predictive validity of SAT scores and high school grade-point average. *Journal of Educational Measurement, 48*(2), 101-121.

ABOUT THE AUTHORS

ELAINE M. ALLENSWORTH is the Lewis-Sebring Director of the University of Chicago Consortium on School Research, where she conducts studies on students' educational attainment, school leadership, and school organization. Her research on high school graduation has been used to create early warning indicator systems in school districts across the country. She is one of the authors of the book, *Organizing Schools for Improvement: Lessons from Chicago*, which documents the ways in which organizational structures in schools influence improvements in student achievement. Dr. Allensworth has received grants from funders that include the Institute of Education Sciences, the National Science Foundation, and the Bill & Melinda Gates Foundation. She frequently works with policymakers and practitioners to bridge research and practice, serving on panels, policy commissions, working groups, and review panels at the local, state, and national level, including the U.S. Department of Education, National Academies, and National Governors' Association. Dr. Allensworth has received a number of awards from the American Educational Research Association for outstanding publications. She has briefed members of congress and their staffers on Consortium research findings, through private meetings, briefings, and congressional testimony. Her work is frequently covered in the local and national media, including the *New York Times*, *Ed Week*, *Chicago Tribune*, public radio, and *CNN*.

JENNY NAGAOKA is the Deputy Director of the UChicago Consortium, where she has conducted research for nearly 20 years. Her research interests focus on policy and practice in urban education reform, particularly using data to connect research and practice and examining the school environments and instructional practices that promote college readiness and success. She has co-authored numerous journal articles and reports, including studies of college readiness, noncognitive factors, the transition from high school to post-secondary education, and authentic intellectual instruction. She is the lead researcher on the To&Through Project, a project that provides educators, policymakers, and families with research, data, and training on the milestones that matter most for college success. Nagaoka is the lead author of *Foundations for Young Adult Success: A Developmental Framework* (2015), which draws on research and practice evidence to build a coherent framework of the foundational factors for young adult success, and investigates their development from early childhood through young adulthood and how they can be supported through developmental experiences and relationships. Nagaoka received her BA from Macalester College and her master's degree in public policy from the Irving B. Harris School of Public Policy at the University of Chicago.

DAVID W. JOHNSON is a Senior Research Analyst at the University of Chicago Consortium on School Research. His research interests focus on school culture and climate, school improvement and processes of institutional change, and postsecondary access and attainment for urban students. His dissertation research focuses on how high schools become socially organized to improve college-going among low-income, minority, and first-generation college students. Johnson holds an AM from the University of Chicago School of Social Service Administration and an MDiv from the University of Chicago Divinity School, as well as an BA from Washington University in St. Louis. Prior to joining the UChicago Consortium, Johnson taught elementary school in the Washington DC Public Schools.

This report reflects the interpretation of the authors. Although the UChicago Consortium's Steering Committee provided technical advice, no formal endorsement by these individuals, organizations, or the full UChicago Consortium should be assumed.

www.ingramcontent.com/pod-product-compliance
Lightning Source LLC
Chambersburg PA
CBHW042126040426

42450CB00002B/85